Cowgirl Devotion

The Revelation

Written by

Jamie Ann Dearing

Photography by

Ruby Lee Langley

Miss Sue! Thank you for Believing in me and for your support! I am grateful for you! 2022 is Greater! Ephesians 3:22 Exceedingly, Abundantly, Above ALL we can dream!

Jamie Ann Dearing ♡†

We would like to dedicate this book to our families who have helped encourage us in this project, especially to Mary Lou Langley, our CHAMPION who has been a constant source of inspiration battling a rare cancer, major back surgery and lives every day legally blind. You are a true witness and a living example of what a 'more than overcomer in Christ Jesus' looks like. Your faith, courage, strength and endurance of the challenges of life are a blessing to all those around you. Thank you for your Godly example.
May the Name of Jesus be continually glorified and magnified in all we say and do!

We Love You,

Jamie & Ruby

1

John 3:16; "For God so loved the world that He gave His only begotten

Son, that whoever believes in Him should not perish but have everlasting life."

This was the very first scripture verse I memorized as a child. Most of us have heard it and many of us have memorized it, but have we truly allowed these words to dwell and permeate our hearts and spirits? God loves YOU (insert your name here)....He loved YOU (insert your name here) so much that He gave His one and only Son so that YOU would not perish but have everlasting life. This promise is for YOU! Your Heavenly Father LOVES YOU, JESUS LOVES YOU - HE DIED FOR YOU! That is a beautiful revelation to receive and walk in my friend!

2 Ephesians 1:3-12; 3 Blessed be the God and Father of our Lord Jesus Christ, who has blessed us with every spiritual blessing in the heavenly places in Christ, 4 just as He chose us in Him before the foundation of the world, that we should be holy and without blame before Him in love, 5 having predestined us to adoption as sons by Jesus Christ to Himself, according to the good pleasure of His will, 6 to the praise of the glory of His grace, by which He made us accepted in the Beloved. 7 In Him we have redemption through His blood, the forgiveness of sins, according to the riches of His grace 8 which He made to abound toward us in all wisdom and prudence, 9 having made known to us the mystery of His will, according to His good pleasure which He purposed in Himself, 10 that in the dispensation of the fullness of the times He might gather together in one all things in Christ, both which are in heaven and which are on earth--in Him. 11 In Him also we have obtained an inheritance, being predestined according to the purpose of Him who works all things according to the counsel of His will, 12 that we who first trusted in Christ should be to the praise of His glory."

We need to realize and choose to believe that God loves us so very much that He has already blessed us with every spiritual blessing in the heavenly places in Christ. To me this is a powerful revelation. I've tried so hard all my life to "earn God's love and blessings" not realizing that I ALREADY HAVE them! Another revelation for us to receive is that God CHOSE US IN HIM BEFORE THE FOUNDATION OF THE WORLD, THAT WE SHOULD BE HOLY AND WITHOUT BLAME BEFORE HIM IN LOVE! WOW! How incredible is that? I chose to believe that I was unworthy, unloved, and was burdened with the feelings of guilt and shame for things that happened to me in my childhood and for poor choices I have made in my adulthood. I chose to believe those lies that the enemy placed in my head that I was no good instead of believing the promises of God. Life gets complicated and it comes at us hard. Life is hard, but God truly is good and He desires for us to live in the freedom and the abundance of what He promises us. The Bible isn't just a storybook of history. It is God's Holy Word. We truly can trust what it says. If you are struggling in your life because of circumstances that have happened to you that were beyond your control, or you are feeling overwhelmed by the guilt and shame of poor choices you've made and are facing the consequences of those choices, I want to encourage you – you have been chosen by God before the foundation of the world that you are to be without blame and that He loves you. He desires to have a relationship with you. He desires for you to have freedom, not be locked in some internal prison of blame, guilt and shame. Stop beating yourself up, take the boot from out of your hind end and talk to God. Pray for forgiveness and thank Him for what He has done for you and ask Him to help you stand on the promises written in His word. Cowgirls are a courageous breed of women. You already have the courage to overcome and accomplish so much. Be courageous in overcoming the battle of your mind – believe in your heart that Jesus Christ is your Lord and Savior. Surrender your life to Him.

3

Psalm 139 1-12:

1 O Lord, you have examined my heart and know everything about me. 2 You know when I sit down or stand up. You know my every thought when far away. 3 You chart the path ahead of me and tell me where to stop and rest. Every moment you know where I am. 4 You know what I am going to say even before I say it, Lord. 5 You both precede and follow me. You place your hand of blessing on my head. 6 Such knowledge is too wonderful for me, too great for me to know! 7 I can never escape from your spirit! I can never get away from your presence! 8 If I go up to heaven, you are there; if I go down to the place of the dead, you are there. 9 If I ride the wings of the morning, if I dwell by the farthest oceans, 10 even there your hand will guide me, and your strength will support me. 11 I could ask the darkness to hide me and the light around me to become night -- 12 but even in darkness I cannot hide from you. To you the night shines as bright as day. Darkness and light are both alike to you.

What an incredible revelation for you to receive today! God knows EVERYTHING about YOU! EVERYTHING!!! Whether you realize it or not God is with you. He knows your every thought. He charts out a path ahead of you; He has a plan for you and knows every moment where you are. He knows what you're going to say before you even say it. God loves you. He has placed His hand of blessing on your head. This is His truth for you to stand on today. In this moment whether you are facing difficulty, confusion, doubt or it is filled with anticipation of the excitement for what's ahead, God is with you. He is there guiding you and strengthening you – all you have to do is RECEIVE. Make a choice today to trust God's Word for your life. Make a choice to receive His love and His help. Make a choice to be LOVED and BLESSED!

Psalm 139: 13-24

13 You made all the delicate, inner parts of my body and knit me together in my mother's womb. 14 Thank you for making me so wonderfully complex! Your workmanship is marvelous -- and how well I know it. 15 You watched me as I was being formed in utter seclusion, as I was woven together in the dark of the womb. 16 You saw me before I was born. Every day of my life was recorded in your book. Every moment was laid out before a single day had passed. 17 How precious are your thoughts about me, O God! They are innumerable! 18 I can't even count them; they outnumber the grains of sand! And when I wake up in the morning, you are still with me!

The day you were born was an amazing day on earth and in heaven! God brought forth His plan to begin your life. It manifested His plan that He began from the foundation of the world to create you. Before you were conceived God had a plan for your life. You are precious to Him. He made all of the delicate inner parts of your body and knit you together in your mother's womb. He designed you, uniquely special to be you. Before you were even born He saw you. Every day of your life was recorded in His book. Every moment of your life was laid out before a single day had passed as you were being formed those months in your mother's womb. God's thoughts of you are precious; they are innumerable! Every morning when you wake up God is with you. Allow these words to be a revelation to you today of just how much your Heavenly Father loves you. He cares about everything you're going through. Whatever you're facing be it joy or pain He knows; it isn't a surprise to Him. Seek Him and ask for His help. Trust Him to help guide you through it. Lean on Him and praise Him for what He has already done and what He can and will do for you!

5

Mark 10:27 But Jesus looked at them and said, "With men it is impossible, but not with God; for with God all things are possible."

Let's review these words. Jesus said, "With men it is impossible, but not with God; for with God all things are possible." This is an incredible nugget of scripture to stand upon for your life today. FOR WITH GOD ALL THINGS ARE POSSIBLE. In our Western way of life we experience many hardships as the life of a cowgirl. We are also blessed to share many great experiences of peace and joy – riding on an open range with the smell of sweet grass and clean air or the thrill of competing in the rodeo arena with thousands cheering for your victory. God is with you. Whatever you are facing today remind yourself of this truth. God loves you and is with you today and always and with God, ALL things truly are possible.

This picture is one of my dearest friends, Mary Lou Langley. Mary Lou is legally blind. This shot was taken by her daughter Ruby five months after major back surgery. The surgeon had to literally build a cage to hold her lower lumbar vertebra in place. Four years prior she had a rare cancer and had to have a complete hysterectomy. She has overcome more in the past five years than most people have experienced in a life time. With true cowgirl grit; courage, faith, and determination, Mary Lou lives this verse out loud. Whatever you are facing today remind yourself of this truth. God loves you and is with you today and always. With God, all things truly are possible.

6

Proverbs 3: 5 & 6 Trust in the LORD with all your heart; do not depend on your own understanding. Seek His will in all you do, and He will direct your paths.

This scripture has seen me through many dark and uncertain days. Our Heavenly Father won't disappoint us. He will always move us in the direction He wants us to be in - and that's not necessarily our plan that we can tangibly understand. Being conflicted means we're standing at a crossroads needing to make a choice. God's Word tells us if we need wisdom to ASK! It's that simple. We don't have to stress ourselves out figuring it all out and figuring out all the back-up plans and their backup plans. I tend to analyze everything – I'm realizing now I just need to give it to God. When I fail and fall I just ask Him for His hand to help me up. My struggles have taught me I need a Savior, I need a friend, I need my Heavenly Father's help - doing it my way is often disastrous - doing it God's way is so much more fruitful and rewarding. I thought being strong meant having to figure it all out for myself. Being strong is letting go and letting God be God, allowing Him to work in and through me. To me, that is the true definition of the term "Cowgirl Up!"

7

Colossians 1:9 - 14 "For this reason we also, since the day we heard it, do not cease to pray for you, and to ask that you may be filled with the knowledge of His will in all wisdom and spiritual understanding; 10 that you may walk worthy of the Lord, fully pleasing Him, being fruitful in every good work and increasing in the knowledge of God; 11 strengthened with all might, according to His glorious power, for all patience and longsuffering with joy; 12 giving thanks to the Father who has qualified us to be partakers of the inheritance of the saints in the light. 13 He has delivered us from the power of darkness and conveyed us into the kingdom of the Son of His love, 14 in whom we have redemption through His blood, the forgiveness of sins."

God desires us to grow, be wise and be strengthened in our spiritual understanding. It is a revelation to think God loves you so much that He has delivered us from the power of darkness. You are redeemed by His blood. You are forgiven. Your Heavenly Father has qualified you to be partakers of the inheritance of the saints in the light. Choose to allow this revelation to dwell deep in your spirit. We are not perfect; we all fall short of the glorious standard of God. Every day is another step in our life's journey and an opportunity to either grow or digress. Choose to live life full out today, giving thanks to God for loving you. You are worthy of His love. You are worthy of His forgiveness and redemption. You are His remarkable creation!

8

Psalm 23 1 A psalm of David. The LORD is my shepherd; I have everything I need. 2 He lets me rest in green meadows; He leads me beside peaceful streams. 3 He renews my strength. He guides me along right paths, bringing honor to His name. 4 Even when I walk through the dark valley of death, I will not be afraid, for you are close beside me. Your rod and your staff protect and comfort me. 5 You prepare a feast for me in the presence of my enemies. You welcome me as a guest, anointing my head with oil. My cup overflows with blessings. 6 Surely your goodness and unfailing love will pursue me all the days of my life, and I will live in the house of the LORD forever.

Allow these words to sink into your spirit. Think about them and choose to allow them to be a healing balm to nurse wherever you are hurting. This verse has been a tremendous blessing to me through the years. It was the second full verse of the Bible I ever learned at the tender age of 6 when I asked Jesus Christ to become my Lord and Savior. I didn't know then what a true life preserver it would be, but the Lord certainly knew what He was doing! Whenever I have been overwhelmed, frustrated, depressed, anxious, frightened, terrified, desperate, lonely, devastated, abandoned, worried, lost, numb, confused, guilty, or shamed, the Holy Spirit has brought this verse to my mind to help me and save me. There have been so many times when I thought I just couldn't live one more moment, walk one more step or breathe one more breath, these words restored me and helped me walk through and overcome that circumstance. When you're hurting you find yourself thinking, "I'll never get out of this, it's hopeless, I can't go on." If you're feeling that way today, stop, take a moment and take a deep breath. Make a choice to change. Stop focusing on the circumstance and the problem. Take a moment to read this verse over several times and allow it to minister to your heart, your mind, and dwell in your spirit. There is hope in God's Word. There is help in God's Word. There is healing in God's Word. There is restoration for your precious life in God's Word; it is His promise to YOU!

9

Matthew 6: 33; But seek first the kingdom of God and His righteousness, and all these things shall be added to you.

Cowgirls by nature are tough and strong. I've had the blessed privilege of living the Western way of life since birth. I was a third generation rodeo competitor and grew up helping my uncle on his ranch and feedlot. My grandparents owned one of New Mexico's largest cattle transportation companies. In my first marriage I managed a feedlot and help operate a sale yard in Oregon. I've seen a great deal of manure, been covered with it and stood knee deep in it. Life can come at us hard and smell like manure. We have a choice to make; continually choosing to struggle with life creating difficulty or to grow and learn and make it better. We choose to make it hard, especially when we choose to resist when God is moving us in the direction of our destiny. God wants to help us in our lives. He wants to bring us out of the muck and the mire and bless us abundantly. The choice is simple; seek first the kingdom of God and His righteousness, and these things shall be added to you. Choose God's way!

10 Psalm 40: 1-5

1 "I waited patiently for the LORD to help me, and He turned to me and heard my cry. 2 He lifted me out of the pit of despair, out of the mud and the mire. He set my feet on solid ground and steadied me as I walked along. 3 He has given me a new song to sing, a hymn of praise to our God. Many will see what He has done and be astounded. They will put their trust in the LORD. 4 Oh, the joys of those who trust the LORD, who have no confidence in the proud, or in those who worship idols. 5 O LORD my God, you have done many miracles for us. Your plans for us are too numerous to list. If I tried to recite all your wonderful deeds, I would never come to the end of them."

What a wonderful truth today! God is here to help you, He hears your cry and He is there to pull you out of the mud and the mire and set your feet on solid ground and steady you as you walk along this journey we call life. He has given you a new song to sing, a hymn of praise to our God. For some of you that's a difficult notion to conceive. You're not knee deep in the muck and mire; it's coming up past your eyeballs and you're drowning in it. Life can be overwhelming at times. I have experienced disappointments, failures, tragedies, and hardships. Each time the Lord faithfully lifted me out of the mess and gave me victory and a new song to sing. He wants to do that for you as well if you will believe in Him and trust Him. We have a lot of old records playing in our heads keeping us from our destiny and living a life of abundance and victory God wants us to live. Our broken record repeats in our head, "You're not good enough." "You're not smart enough." "You don't have any talent." "You're not strong enough." "You're not pretty." "You're fat." "You're ugly." "You're too skinny." "You're too sensitive." "You're angry." "You're rude." "You're mean." "You're hateful." The list goes on and on, playing over and over in your subconscious keeping us locked in a prison of self-doubt. It's time to break those records! It's time to write new ones and sing new songs of praise to our God. He has created you unique and beautiful. You are His remarkable creation. Choose today not to listen to the broken records – the lies the enemy puts in your head to make you defeat yourself and God's purpose for you. Oh, the joys of those who trust the LORD! His plans for you are too numerous to list.

11

Psalm 27:1-5 1 A psalm of David. The LORD is my light and my salvation -- so why should I be afraid? The LORD protects me from danger -- so why should I tremble? 2 When evil people come to destroy me, when my enemies and foes attack me, they will stumble and fall. 3 Though a mighty army surrounds me, my heart will know no fear. Even if they attack me, I remain confident. 4 The one thing I ask of the LORD -- the thing I seek most -- is to live in the house of the LORD all the days of my life, delighting in the LORD's perfections and meditating in His Temple. 5 For He will conceal me there when troubles come; He will hide me in His sanctuary. He will place me out of reach on a high rock.

God wants to protect us. He wants to become our sanctuary where He can conceal us in the times of trouble. Imagine yourself today crawling in His lap and seeking His comforting arms to restore you. Even when we are being attacked, this scripture promises us we can remain CONFIDENT. We can be focused, peaceful, grounded and centered knowing that God is protecting us. It's our choice how we choose to show up in the moment! Praise the Lord!

12

Nehemiah 8:10 – "Don't be dejected and sad, for the joy of the LORD is your strength."

We truly have so much to be thankful for, yet the world is constantly trying to steal our joy. Most of the time, we choose to give it away by the choices we make. People have shared this verse with me to cheer me up in tough situations when I was angry, dejected, or sad. I never truly appreciated this portion of God's Word until recently. I discovered that anger is a mechanism we use when we are in resistance to something. Most of the time we are resistant to change, even if that change is better for us; moving us into the place we need to be to accomplish our purpose in life. The revelation of this hit me pretty hard because I've always used the excuse that I'm part Irish and part Scottish and getting angry quickly, or "having a short fuse" is just part of my personality. God's Word instructs us to be SLOW to anger. I always had a tendency to react negatively. If things didn't go my way I would allow my emotions to control me and my circumstances. I would lose control and have no strength left in me. It's vital for our well being; physically, mentally, and spiritually to make better choices and to recognize that God's Word is the best instruction manual for life we could as for! Ask yourself, why am I sad, dejected, and angry? I have discovered that when we hold on to unforgiveness we stuff the disappointments, the rejections and pain, not recognizing that all of that junk rests in our subconscious (spirit) and actually contributes to our poor choices. Joy in the Lord is truly our strength. We can't be filled up with all the good things living full out in the purpose God has for us when we are filled with the bitter disappointments of the past. God has a destiny for each one of us to accomplish. I encourage you to begin today by standing on the promises of God's Word. Renew your mind and seek help and counsel to reconcile and heal the past. If you want more joy and peace in your life, be around positive people that build you up and fill you full of joy. Be committed to living life from a positive and joyful perspective. We truly have so much to be thankful for!

13

Joshua 1: 9 "I command you — be strong and courageous! Do not be afraid or discouraged. For the LORD your God is with you wherever you go."

It is a great comfort to me to know that God promises us that 'He is with us wherever you go!' How often do we instantly react negatively to a situation and allow our emotions to take over, choosing to listening to that old record in our heads that we "CAN'T", "WATCH OUT FOR THIS", "WATCH OUT FOR THAT", "IT'S IMPOSSIBLE", "YOU DON'T DESERVE THAT", "IT'S TOO HARD", "YOU CAN'T TRUST THEM"...etc., etc. I encourage you today to get rid of that old record player. Choose to commit to yourself that YOU ARE ABLE AND THAT WITH GOD ALL THINGS ARE POSSIBLE!!! Commit to telling yourself that you are STRONG AND COURAGEOUS! When the devil comes in with his bag of hot air and lies rebuke him with your words and say out loud, "I AM STRONG AND COURAGEOUS, FOR THE LORD MY GOD IS WITH ME WHEREVER I GO!" Encourage yourself and think positive. Choose to be joyful and happy. Take a few deep breaths and say this verse several times and watch your circumstances and attitude shift for the better! God loves you and no matter what you're going through, He is with you wherever you go!

14

Psalm 50: 10-15 "For all the animals of the forest are mine and I own the cattle on a thousand hills. Every bird of the mountains and all the animals of the field belong to me. If I were hungry, I would not mention it to you, for all the world is mine and everything in it. I don't need the bulls you sacrifice; I don't need the blood of goats. What I want instead is your true thanks to God; I want you to fulfill your vows to the Most High. Trust in me in your times of trouble, and I will rescue you, and you will give me glory."

As cowgirls, it might be difficult for many of us to even imagine in our minds the magnitude of God owning the cattle on a thousand hills….or that every bird in the forest and field, every bird belongs to Him. God is the Creator of all. He has authority over everything. This scripture speaks to me of His power and authority. It is important to choose to commit ourselves to develop a deep personal relationship with Jesus Christ. God is not concerned about the sacrifices we make for Him, or the works we can get caught up in trying to impress others by conforming to religious standards. It's not about religion, it's about relationship. This scripture encourages us to trust in Him in times of trouble. He's there to rescue you. He wants to give you glory. What a wonderful truth to stand on today! God already knows what the outcome will be. It's our choice whether or not we want to suffer in the present circumstance or choose to trust God to rescue us. He loves you and is there with all the answers to rescue you and help give you the glory. Trust Him for your life and allow Jesus to work in and through you.

15

Psalm 51: 10-12 "Create in me a clean heart, O God. Renew a right spirit within me. Do not banish me from your presence and don't take your Holy Spirit from me. Restore to me again the joy of your salvation and make me willing to obey you."

Life can be a great blessing as well as a tremendous challenge. It has been my experience that there are many trials and tribulations to teach us wonderful life lessons and mold our character, renew our minds, and change our lives, but there are few of the true glory moments that we celebrate the victories. I believe that our true character is revealed in the challenges. We decide then how we show up. I don't believe we can truly appreciate any of the lessons God designed uniquely for us when we choose to allow ourselves to close our hearts off to His teaching. We are locked deep in a self-imposed prison of unforgiveness, resentment, blame, shame or guilt. The cry of our hearts every day needs to be this prayer; "Create in me a clean heart, Oh God. Renew a right spirit within me. Do not banish me from your presence and don't take your Holy Spirit from me. Restore to me again the joy of your salvation and make me willing to obey you, renewing a right spirit within me." When we allow ourselves to truly live this prayer we will be free from the resistance. We then are cooperating with God and able to face the challenges with greater strength and faith that God is truly in control, leading us to His true purpose and destiny.

16

Psalm 18: 1-6 "I love you, LORD; you are my strength. The LORD is my rock, my fortress, and my savior; my God is my rock in whom I find protection. He is my shield the strength of my salvation, and my stronghold. I will call on the LORD who is worthy of praise, for He saves me from my enemies. The ropes of death surrounded me; death itself stared me in the face. But in my distress I cried out to the LORD; yes, I prayed to my God for help. He heard me from His sanctuary; my cry reached His ears."

Cowgirls are a strong, independent breed of women. We like to do things on our own. During my dark days I felt as though I had to prove to the world that I was capable of getting through the situation on my own. I convinced myself that I didn't need anything or anybody. This attitude was formed from experiences of pain and hurt; from places of betrayal and abuse. I had developed a relentless victim mentality. When I was unable to succeed at whatever I was trying to accomplish, I blamed others for my plight. The broken record that played in my head was, "Why has this happened to me? God must not love me! No one loves me, no one cares about me. I am unlovable. No one wants ME! Why would they? I am miserable and my life is miserable. I don't matter." Those negative words played in my head as I enjoyed my self-inflicted pity party making things worse; contributing to the problem and increasing the pain.

I remember one night crying out to God for help as death stared me in the face, begging Him to save me. You are reading this book as a result of that answered prayer! PRAISE GOD! God truly heard my cry and began directing me towards a more positive direction, propelling me forward to my destiny. He placed people along my path to help support me. They showed me what love is and gave me hope of a better life. I quickly learned that I needed support and that I was not weak or incapable if I received help.

We choose to stay stuck in misery when we continue to believe the lies of the enemy, believing that we don't need help, love, and support. The devil wants to keep you secluded by yourself. He wants you to be miserable. He wants to keep you from happiness and the victory of receiving your destiny. HE IS A LIAR!

I want to encourage you today; put on your new record of praise and thanksgiving to God. Even if it a struggle to do so, you will see an instant shift in your attitude and in your spirit. Do not choose to listen to the lies of the enemy. Ignore that noise and focus on what God's Word assures you.

Pray this prayer, "I love you Lord, You are my rock, my fortress, and my savior; my God is my rock in whom I find protection. You are my shield the strength of my salvation, and my stronghold. My Lord, you are worthy of praise." Pray this over and over, believe and trust that God will hear you from His sanctuary and answer your prayer. He has answered my prayers and I trust He will answer yours as well! You are just one prayer and one choice away from moving towards your destiny!

17 James 1: 2-4 "Dear brothers and sisters, whenever trouble comes your way, be an opportunity for joy. For when your faith is tested, your endurance has a chance to grow. So let it grow for when your endurance is fully developed, you will be strong in character and ready for anything."

I remember the first time I read this scripture and heard a message taught about it. I was going through a horrendous divorce, full of guilt and shame for the choices I made. My two small children and I lived in an old drafty mobile home. Sometimes I had to choose whether to pay the electric bill or scrap together money for groceries. I would scrounge money sometimes from my kids' piggy banks to treat them to McDonalds filling the bags with extra ketchup that I later used to make tomato soup and spaghetti sauce with. As my Mother had often said to me growing up, "I'm so broke I can't even pay attention." I felt that everything about my life was broken. The darkness that surrounded me engulfed me like a shroud. My mind was numb, I existed on auto pilot. My thoughts were filled with all the guilt, the shame, and blame for every poor choice and mistake I had ever made. When I read these words I wanted to laugh out loud. I thought to myself, "Yeah right God how am I supposed to have joy when I can't even conceive the concept of that word. Really? Don't you know what I've been through in my life? Don't you know what I've done and what was done to me? Are you kidding me, so what does JOY even look like?"

Looking back now many years on the other side of that circumstance, I see how God used this verse to minister to my life. After church that day I remember taking my children to the park and marveling at the joy and innocence of their wonderment of the world. Every new discovery was a joyful experience. As they laughed and played I found myself joining them. As we rolled in

the grass and laughed, the Lord began restoring my hope and gave me a glimpse of what joy was: feeling the warmth of their hugs and seeing the love in their eyes. Each new day, as I began to put my trust in the Lord, He continued to restore my life as I considered the joy in every new moment. He placed people all along my path to help me, support me, love me, and teach me joy. Two of the greatest blessings I've ever known are my children Brady and KayCee. They have been the greatest teachers of my life. They are grown now with beautiful children of their own. I marvel at the beauty of my grandsons Rowdy and Cooper. Our family truly has endured a great deal. Our faith has been stretched and tested beyond belief. The Lord has been there every step of the way. I know now nearly 20 years later that as our faith and character continues to grow as a person and as a family it is essential for our further growth to always choose to focus on the joy of the moment. Fixing your eyes on Jesus and the blessings helps you get through your darkest of days. Choose joy, choose peace, choose happiness, choose Jesus.

I want to encourage you today, when you are facing a trial or a difficult situation or circumstances, consider the joy in the moment. God gives us the free will to make our choices, but even when we've chosen to make a wrong decision, His grace is greater. God's Word assures us that He works all things for our good. Most of the time we can't even begin to understand why we go through the things we go through. It's not until we are on the other side of the storm that we can marvel at its beauty and the lessons that we learned. God has a purpose for everything He allows us to go through. He wants to grow our faith and strength so that we truly will be ready for anything. He uses our circumstances to minister to us and strengthen our character and faith. He ministers to others that are witnessing our reactions in the circumstance as well. God has a method to what is seemingly madness; it is truly for our good. We might not be able to see it in the moment…..we will down the road. There is always joy in every situation, focus on that, hang on to the promises in God's Word, He WILL see you through.

18

Hebrews 12:12 "So take a new grip with your tired hands and stand firm on your shaky legs. Mark out a straight path for your feet. Then those who follow you, though they are weak and lame, will not stumble and fall but will become strong."

You've probably heard the saying, "Get a grip!" That's what all of us need to do when life begins spinning out of control. Sometimes we have been battling in a circumstance for so long that we need to get a new grip, take a FIRM stand. We get lost in the circumstance and take bunny trails away from our destiny. This scripture reminds us to mark out a straight path for our feet. We have people all around us in our sphere of influence following our every move. Some are stronger than us in our walk with the Lord, and others are not as strong. It's important that we are personally responsible for the reactions, the choices, the attitudes, the words we speak, and for the manners that we have. When we are not living by faith and not choosing to walk in integrity and according to God's Word, we may be a negative influence to someone following us. It's important to do our best each and every day to choose wisely so that those following us do not stumble and fall but will become strong in their walk because of our influence. We have a responsibility to ourselves, to others and to the Lord as to how we choose to live this life!

19

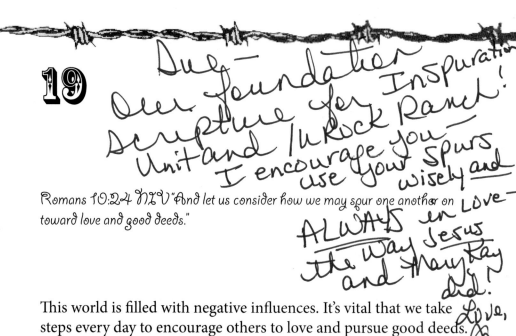

Dee —
Our foundation scripture for Inspiration!
Unit and /U Rock Ranch —
I encourage you use your spurs wisely and ALWAYS in LOVE — the way Jesus and Mary Kay did!

Love,
Pam
12-13-21

Romans 10:24 *NIV* "And let us consider how we may spur one another on toward love and good deeds."

This world is filled with negative influences. It's vital that we take steps every day to encourage others to love and pursue good deeds. We can choose to get lost in the noise and conflict, the drama and heartache of the pain. We can choose to listen to the broken record playing in our head that we aren't enough. We can choose to follow along with the world and its poisonous and toxic standards, status, and stigmas or we can choose to believe the promises written in God's Word for our lives and truly make a difference in this world. Encourage and SPUR the people that God places in your life. Respect them, honor them, genuinely care about them, be kind and compassionate to them, and treat yourself with respect and honor. If we all make an effort to do this on a daily basis, I believe our world would become a better place. As cowgirls we know how to spur a horse to encourage it to go faster – let's put our spurs to a different use – encouraging ourselves and others towards love and good deeds. Let's unite together in this cause and create a better world! COMPASSIONATE COWGIRLS UNITED IN GOD'S POWER!

20

1 Corinthians 14: 4-7 "Love is patient and kind. Love is not jealous or boastful or proud or rude. Love does not demand its own way. Love is not irritable and it keeps no record of when it has been wronged. It is never glad about injustice but rejoices whenever the truth wins out. Love never gives up, never loses faith, is always hopeful, and endures through every circumstance."

The solution and answer to all the problems of this world – LOVE! If we truly focus on loving God, being obedient to His Word, loving others, and loving ourselves, our lives would be less stressful and complicated. We would experience greater peace and joy. Allow this scripture to indwell in our hearts and minds every day and focus on love. We will create a better world.

21

2 Corinthians 12:9 Each time He said, "My gracious favor is all you need. My power works best in your weakness." So now I am glad to boast about my weaknesses, so that the power of Christ may work through me.

In our weakness He is strong. None of us wants to be a failure or admit that we have failed. We hate the feeling of brokenness and emptiness. How can God ever truly bring healing into our lives and fill us to the overflowing measure that He intends for us if we are constantly trying to be tough and be strong? Cowgirls are a strong and tough breed of women. We don't want to admit our weaknesses because we have had it ingrained in us it is failure in itself. By nature a cowgirl must be strong both physically and emotionally to be able to handle the challenges of life, however GOD wants us to rely on HIM to be our strength. The more we resist God pulling at our hearts and trying to figure it all out on our own, the harder life will be for us. When we can come to the place of understanding that God loves us so much that all He wants is to take away our pain, our hurts, brokenness and emptiness so that He can heal us, HE can comfort us, and HE can fill us with HIS love, only then we will have the breakthrough we need.

This has been a huge revelation for me because I never felt worthy of God's love. I've had this broken record playing in my head since childhood telling me that "I am a failure, that I'll never amount to anything, that I don't matter, I am nothing special, that I'm not worthy" – those are lies that I've chosen to believe straight from the pit of hell! God's Word tells me that He loves me. That He has a plan to prosper me to give me a future and a hope, that I am the BELOVED child that without God in my life I am and always will be a miserable failure. I had to learn to surrender myself and admit that I was a failure that I am a failure without Him but with Him I truly can do all things. God makes me powerful when I surrender my will to Him. In my weakness He is strong. I pray that you will receive this truth for your life. I pray that you are receiving a revelation today that NONE of us are worthy of God's love, but through His grace and love we are made to be daughters of the Most High, the King of Kings and Lord of Lords, the Mighty Creator of the Universe. It's time to break those old records playing in our heads with the lies and write new records to remind ourselves each and every day of who we are in Christ Jesus! You are BELOVED, PRECIOUS, AND UNIQUELY BEAUTIFUL CREATION made by God! He believes, you are BEAUTIFUL, you are STRONG, you are POWERFUL, you are WORTHY, you are CAPABLE, you are LOVING, you are KIND, you are SMART, you are TALENTED, you are AMAZING, you are INCREDIBLE, now give yourself permission to BELIEVE IN YOURSELF and tell yourself these words of affirmation every day until it is ingrained into and dwells in your spirit. Choose to break the old records and choose to write a new record for your life – a song based on the truth of God's Word of who you are in Christ. You were created to be loved by God!

22

Psalm 70:4 Let all those who seek you rejoice and be glad in you;

And let those who love Your salvation say continually, "Let God be magnified!"

We live in a world that can often times rob of us of our happiness; steal our love and our hope. People are going to disappoint us. We choose in the moment how we are going to react. We choose to be hurt and allow bitterness in, or we choose to let things go and for God to work them out, every moment we have a CHOICE. We are going to be misunderstood. We are going to be judged whether we like it or not. Quite simply, life is hard! God, however is GOOD, and He is good ALL THE TIME!!!

I've been a Christian the majority of my life. As I've shared, I accepted Christ as my personal Lord and Savior at the tender age of 6 years old. I haven't always walked with God throughout this journey of life. I've made my share of poor choices and mistakes as we all do. One thing my Mom has always taught me is that you do the best you can do one day at a time, that's all you can do. I know now as an adult to take that advice to heart as I trust God to help me do the best that I can instead of relying on my own strength and understanding. One thing I know for sure without a shadow of a doubt, God has always been walking with me. Sometimes He has carried me when I didn't even realize it, comforting me and providing for me in ways I couldn't even imagine. He's ALWAYS and FAITHFULLY been there for me.

Recently I've had a huge revelation of my Heavenly Father and His love for me. I want to share this experience with you. God loves you! When the world is crashing down around you He's standing right there with loving arms wanting us to accept His comfort and grace. All we have to do is surrender and pray. Some situations and challenges in life are so great we don't have any words. When I go through these times, I just say one word - "JESUS!" Our new song that we must choose to sing is rejoicing in God, being glad in Him, "Let the Lord be glorified, let His name be praised and magnified." When we keep this mindset we will see a drastic shift of change for the better in our lives.

23

Romans 12:2. Don't copy the behavior and customs of this world, but let God transform you into a new person by changing the way you think. Then you will know what God wants you to do, and you will know how good and pleasing and perfect His will really is.

This scripture is a great reminder that we do not have to choose to live according to the standards of this world. When we choose to live by the promises and the standards written in God's Word and allow God to transform us into the new person He desires us to be, we will truly have the victory for our lives that we desire. It's difficult for us to stop listening to the broken records playing in our minds that we are not enough. Those broken records are lies from the devil. He is just a bag of hot air! We need to choose to listen to the promises written in God's Word of who we are in Him. Most people don't want to give up what they consider as "pleasures of the world." Most of the time that's just their own selfish sinful nature talking or the broken record playing in their head and they don't even realize it or realize the hold it has on them. When we try to "fit in" the way that everyone else in the secular world thinks, acts or behaves we aren't living the life of freedom, joy and abundance God intends for us to have. We need to think differently than the world. We need to act differently than the world. It's a good thing and it's what God is calling of us to do!

24

James 1:18 In His goodness He chose to make us His own children by giving us His true word. And we, out of all creation, became His choice possession.

What a beautiful revelation today! In His goodness, God has chosen us to make us His own children by giving us His TRUE Word! We, out of ALL Creation, became His CHOICE possession! You are a CHOICE possession to God! Do not allow anyone or anything to tell you otherwise! You are HIS CHILD. His Word is TRUE!! Stand on this today and believe it for your life. YOUR ARE A PRECIOUS, CHOSEN CHILD OF GOD, A CHOICE POSSESSION!

25

Galatians 5:22-23 "But when the Holy Spirit controls our lives He will produce this kind of fruit in us: love, joy, peace, patience, kindness, goodness, faithfulness, gentleness, and self-control. Here there is no conflict with the law."

This scripture has been a huge part of my life for a long time. I have struggled with trying to become all of these things. As I have grown in my walk with the Lord He has begun to transform me and has helped me to develop the fruit of my spirit. I failed miserably when I tried to do it on my own, in my own "religious way." When my kids were growing up and they had moments when they were acting up I would ask them, "How are we supposed to act in this family?" Most of the time I wasn't showing them an example of a true Godly attitude myself! We laugh about it now as they are raising their own children. It was through those difficult times God spoke clearly to my heart that it is important for me to not only "preach the message", but to also "live the message." We must be a living example of God's Word, sharing His love, joy, peace, patience, kindness, goodness, faithfulness, gentleness, and self-control. The world will not teach us these examples. These are the kind of attitudes and behaviors we must all strive for and possess, not just expect everyone else to. We must take personal responsibility each day for our thoughts, words and actions. When we're wrong or act inappropriately, we must quickly recognize it and get ourselves back on track. We'll make our share of mistakes and have our share of bad choices and bad attitudes, we are human. Like any good cowgirl knows, when you get bucked off, you need to pick yourself up, dust yourself off, and get right back in the saddle. God desires for us to be examples of Him, His love and character of compassion.

26

Revelation 10:9-10 "For if you confess with your mouth that Jesus is Lord and believe in your heart that God raised Him from the dead, you will be saved. For it is by believing in your heart that you are made right with God, and it is by confessing with your mouth that you are saved."

Our salvation is simple. All we must do is believe in Jesus Christ in our heart and confess that He is Lord and we will be made right with God. At that moment our sin is forgiven and we are graphed into the inheritance as heirs to the Living King of Kings and Lord of Lords (Hebrews 1:2). All of our sin is washed clean, the Bible tells us in Isaiah 1:18 "No matter how deep the stain of your sins I can remove it. I can make you as clean as freshly fallen snow. Even if you are stained as red as crimson, I can make you white as wool. If you will only obey me and let me help you..." Friends, these are powerful promises for us to trust and stand upon in our lives. God desires for us to have a personal relationship with Him and live with Him forever in eternity. We cannot share in this promise if we do not confess and believe. God truly has created you for a specific purpose to accomplish at a specific time in the history of this world. You are called to be His Child. He loves you so much that as our Heavenly Father He sent His one and only Son to die and suffer for your sins. Receive this revelation today that you deserve a beautiful life here on earth and eternal life in heaven. I pray you give your heart to Him today.

27

2 Corinthians 4: 7-9 "But this precious treasure — this light and power that now shine within us — is held in perishable containers, that is, in our weak bodies. So everyone can see that our glorious power is from God and is not our own. We are pressed on every side by troubles, but we are not crushed or broken. We are perplexed, but don't give up and quit. We are hunted down, but God never abandons us. We get knocked down, but we get up again and keep going."

You are a precious treasure! God truly wants you to believe that. If you struggle to find that difficult to believe I want you to notice that you have an opposite belief system that is not in alignment with God's Word. The devil doesn't want you to believe that you're a PRECIOUS treasure. He lies to you all the time with his constant barrage of broken records playing in your head that "you are not precious, you are not worthy, you don't deserve God's love…after all, how could He with all the bad things you've said and done?" You need to take authority over that broken record in the Name of Jesus and tell the devil to get behind you – take a hike devil! He has absolutely no power or authority in your life! The negative thoughts that play in your head are Satan's way of keeping your from your destiny and the greatness of who you are in Christ. Our minds and our bodies are weak. We are perishable containers, God created us so that everyone can see that our glorious power is from God and is not our own. Through Christ and His power we can do all things! Through Christ's power all things are possible! We will be challenged in this world until the moment we take our last breath. We will have troubles, but we do not have to allow it to crush us or break us down. We will be confused, frustrated and dismayed, we will be perplexed, but we must not give up and quit. God will not abandon you! Allow Jesus to ride in the seat of the saddle, give Him the reigns. Get behind Him and the cantle and hold on tight! He will help you ride successfully through any storm of life no matter how difficult it may be. You are a precious treasure! Believe that and ride STRONG IN CHRIST'S MIGHTY POWER IN AND THROUGH YOU!!!

Romans 8: 26- 30 "And we know that God causes everything to work to-gether for the good of those who love God and are called according to His purpose for them. For God knew His people in advance, and He chose them to become like His Son, so that His Son would be the firstborn, with many brothers and sisters. And having chosen them, He called them to come to Him. And He gave them right standing with Himself, and promised them His glory."

We live in a broken and fallen world where disappointments, fail-ures, and tragedies happen every day. It's difficult to wrap our mind around how and why things happen. When we choose to live in sin we leave an open door for Satan to come in and bring destruc-tion into our lives. Things happen sometimes out of our control, even when we're not choosing to live in sin. You've heard the say-ing, "stuff happens", I'm here to tell you it does. God gave us this scripture as a promise that He causes everything to work together for good for those who love Him and are called accord to His pur-pose for them. Sometimes in our misguided goals and dreams God works things in a different way than we had planned so that we can move in the direction of His will. We shouldn't try so hard to figure it all out. I'm a real analyzer and controlling type of personality, most women are. However, GOD is the one in control. When we get freaked out over life and the circumstances and happenings we need this verse to remind us that there is hope in Christ and that God will work it all out for our good for His purpose for us. We need to trust God and take Him at His Word and wait on His per-fect timing. Responding in God's love instead of reacting out of fear and doubt will get us closer to our destiny.

29

Romans 8: 31-32 "What can we say about such wonderful things as these? If God is for us, who can ever be against us? Since God did not spare even His own Son but gave Him up for us all, won't God, who gave us Christ, also give us everything else?"

I pray that you would allow this verse to renew your mind. When people and circumstance try to knock you down and discourage you, know in your heart and truly believe that if God is for YOU, who can be against YOU? The devil is a little pipsqueak. He is a liar and a thief that desires to destroy you and your purpose. You have a destiny. The devil has no power or authority in your life. You were purchased with a precious price – Jesus gave His life for you so that you have eternal life in heaven AND so that you can live an abundant, peaceful life here on earth. We live in a world that is filled with pain and devastation. We can easily be consumed by all of the temptations and choose to live that way or we can choose the life God has designed for us. God loves you so very much that He gave His one and only Son, Jesus Christ up for you. For every choice we make there is a cost and a benefit. Choose today to let go of the past. Choose today to tell the devil, "I'm not playing this game! You have no power or authority over me. You are a liar and I'm taking my life back. I'm breaking that record and I'm choosing to believe in the promises God has written in His Word for me, if God is for me, who can be against me!" PRAISE AND GLORY BE TO GOD!

30

Romans 8: 33-35 "Who dares accuse us whom God has chosen for His own? Will God? No! He is the one who has given us right standing with Himself. Who then will condemn us? Will Christ Jesus? No, for He is the one who died for us and was raised to life for us and is sitting at the place of highest honor next to God, pleading for us. Can anything ever separate us from Christ's love? Does it mean He no longer loves us if we have trouble or calamity, or are persecuted, or are hungry or cold or in danger or threatened with death? Even the Scriptures say, 'For your sake we are killed every day; we are being slaughtered like sheep.' No despite all these things, overwhelming victory is ours through Christ who loved us."

What an incredibly powerful scripture to stand on today! God has given us right standing with Him. He has chosen you and I to be His very own. No matter what our circumstances, no matter our choices or what happens to us beyond our control God loves us and gave us the gift of salvation in Jesus Christ. Choosing our salvation in Jesus gives us the security that no matter what we go through NOTHING can separate us from the love of God. He has placed Jesus in a place right next to Him in a place of honor and authority. Jesus pleads on our behalf. Isn't that amazing? This scripture promises us that despite all things, OVERWHELMING VICTORY is ours through Christ Jesus! When you find yourself overwhelmed with the world and what you're going through in life, call out to Jesus! Don't call anyone else frustrated, worried, angry or confused. That just gets you stirred up and makes things worse. I encourage you, stand on this scripture today and trust that you will receive overwhelming victory when you trust Jesus. Wait on His timing for the answer. He always has the perfect timing and the perfect answer to help you overcome anything.

31

Romans 8: 38-39 "I am convinced that nothing can ever separate us from His love. Death can't and life can't. The angels can't, and the demons can't. Our fears for today, our worries about tomorrow, and even the powers of hell can't keep God's love away. Whether we are high above the sky or in the deepest ocean, nothing in all creation will ever be able to separate us from the love of God that is revealed in Christ Jesus our Lord."

Allow this scripture to sink deep within your mind and spirit. Read it again several times. God's Word promises here in this verse that NOTHING IN ALL CREATION WILL EVER BE ABLE TO SEPARATE US FROM THE LOVE OF GOD. We fight a great many battles both in the spirit and in our everyday living. We can become bogged down and overwhelmed with it all. Life can quickly steal our joy if we allow it to. I've had days when I couldn't get out of bed because the fear of the day and the worries of tomorrow. I didn't know how to trust in God. It was impossible to think or hope for anything different. God tells us not to fear, yet so many of us are locked in self-imposed prisons of fear and doubt which keep us from pursuing our goals and striving for our destiny. It is comforting to know that God loves us with such boundless love. I encourage you today to choose to stop worrying and living in fear. Choose forgiveness and freedom. The Bible tells us that worry does not add one hour to our day. In reality I believe it robs us of seeing and appreciating the great many blessings placed right before us. I encourage you to make a choice to shift your thinking today and choose to believe that God has you in the palm of His hand leading you to an exciting and rewarding destiny. Don't let anything keep you from the love of God, and remember, nothing separates you from His love.

32

Jeremiah 29:11 "For the thoughts I think toward you, says the Lord, thoughts of peace and not evil, to give you a future and a hope."

God has an amazing plan and destiny for your life. YOU CAN BELIEVE THAT! This scripture is a wonderful encouragement that God Himself has planned your destiny. His desire is to prosper you, to give you a future and a hope. Remember back in our earlier readings in Psalm 139 that God knows every day of your life and has planned it out. Nothing is a surprise to Him. He gives us free will and choice and through His amazing grace and mercy helps direct, guide, and protect us. Beginning at birth our fallen world begins to tear us away from God's plan. Through our environment and experiences we begin to develop belief systems. Some of those belief systems serve us and God's purpose for us; however most of them do not. Words can be so damaging, especially to a child. Someone tells us, "No, you can't do this or that", "You're not capable of doing that", "You're just a baby", "You're too little", "You're too skinny", "You're too tall", "You're too fat", "You're too short", "You're dumb", "You're ugly", "You'll never accomplish that", "I don't care about you", "I don't like you", "You'll never be good enough", "We don't have any money", "We're poor, we can't afford that", "People like us don't deserve that", "It's a sin to have luxury", "Your opinion is not important to me." The list of negative statements goes on and on. These negative statements create belief systems that I refer to as 'broken records'. When we choose to believe these negative statements someone has spoken into our lives we have a difficult time believing anything positive. The broken record just keeps playing over and over in our minds and drowns out everything good and positive. This is a tactic the devil uses to steal our destiny and victory from our lives. He wants us to believe the lies. His desire is to steal truth, steal our joy, steal our hope, and steal our faith. He wants to sear our conscious from all that is moral and true. We willingly give the enemy power over our lives when we choose to believe any negative statement. That's why it is vital to continually feed on God's Word, the living truth, the guide manual for life. We must renew our minds daily. Just as we feed our bodies with food and fuel our cars with gasoline, we must feed our mind and spirit devoting time to reading the Bible daily. It is as equally vital to surround ourselves with people that help encourage and inspire us; people that feed our love tank daily and not suck us dry. A healthy nutritious diet is vital to feeding your body to help you maximize your energy and vitality. God's destiny does not just fall into our laps. He isn't our Fairy God Mother waving a magic wand to make our dreams come true. We must choose to surrender our hearts, our minds, our wills, and our lives to God so that He will release His divine power to bring us to His destiny. All things with God are possible; the first step is to believe God and reject anything contrary to His Word.

33

Philippians 4:8, "...Fix your thoughts on what is TRUE and HON-ORABLE and RIGHT. Think about things that are PURE and LOVELY and ADMIRABLE. Think about things that are EXCELLENT and WOR-THY OF PRAISE."

Most of the thoughts that run through the average person's mind each day are not true, honorable, right, pure, lovely, admirable, excellent, or worthy of praise. We are bombarded every moment of the day with negative information, images, and attitudes through television, radio, newspapers, magazines, billboard advertising, people we come in contact with in the community, and the people in our own sphere of influence who can often be negative and toxic. We need to notice each day what we are allowing into our spirit and into our subconscious. We cannot allow anything to have a negative influence on our life. When we allow our minds to focus on the negative things we develop negative attitudes and become bitter individuals like the rest of the world. We begin to react in negative ways and end up hurting the people we love the most and wind up hurt ourselves. We create a constant state of sabotage because we have then developed a belief system that we are not worthy. We unknowingly hurt ourselves and others always needing to be "right" about our beliefs. In order to heal from this constant state of chaos, we must learn to recognize the negative thoughts, information and influences in our lives. We need to constantly feed our minds with positive thoughts and information. We need to be around like minded positive people that help build us up and stay focused and centered on positive thoughts that are true, honorable, right, pure, lovely, admirable things that are excellent and worthy of praise. As soon as we experience a negative thought, image, or influence we need to change the channel in our minds and focus on something positive. For many people they have no concept of this, they've lived in a negative environment with no love and hope, nothing positive in their world. We need to reach out to these people with the love and promises of God's Word and share hope with them as we continually work on our own thought patterns and attitudes. When we commit to responding in love and concentrating on living responsibly, with positive thoughts and actions we will create a better world. Be a world changer today by staying positive!

34

Psalm 37:4 Take delight in the LORD, and He will give you your heart's desires.

God truly wants us to live an abundant life, He wants to give us the desires of our heart and bless us more than we can possibly think or imagine. I truly believe that the majority of people do not believe that this is possible because they believe in the broken record playing in their head that is telling them, "you are not worthy, you don't deserve it, you are not enough..." I'm here to tell you that those thoughts you are thinking were created by a wrong belief system. To change your life you must change your beliefs you must believe that you ARE ENOUGH – YOU ARE ENOUGH BECAUSE HE IS ENOUGH!!! As you begin to think differently you will begin to create a better attitude about yourself. As you continually strive to affirm yourself and your beliefs you will be able to see more joy and have more peace in your life. We all stuff our problems, conflicts, hurts, and pains in a trash can deep in our subconscious. After years of stuffing our spirit becomes contaminated with all of the hurts, the junk, and it begins to spill over into every aspect of our lives. We become toxic and we then influence everything and everyone around us. That is what I believe is the core for every problem in this world – hurting people hurt people. This is the cause of war, divorce, abuse, crime, neglect, you name it! We need to come to a realization that we need a shift in our belief system. We need to think about more positive things and take control of our lives and what we surround ourselves with in our personal sphere of influence. When we begin to go through the layers of our trash can and allow the Lord to heal us, we then begin to make room for the good things of this world. Not long ago I had a miraculous experience that helped me to see the world in a totally new way. I was able to truly forgive some people that had deeply hurt me. I had carried the pain of unforgiveness and bitterness with me for a long time. I wore the pain like a coat, not realizing how it affected every aspect of my life. The moment I received this revelation and truly walked in forgiveness •• colors were more vibrant, sounds were more clear and beautiful, food tasted better, all of my senses were renewed. Friends, God wants you to be honest with yourself and begin dealing with your trash can. He wants you to truly delight in Him so that He can make the way to give you the desires of your heart. I want to encourage you to trust Him today and begin to walk in a new and renewed life. The life God has purposed you to have!

35

The Armor of God

Ephesians 6:10-18: 10 A final word: Be strong with the Lord's mighty power. 11 Put on all of God's armor so that you will be able to stand firm against all strategies and tricks of the Devil. 12 For we are not fighting against people made of flesh and blood, but against the evil rulers and authorities of the unseen world, against those mighty powers of darkness who rule this world, and against wicked spirits in the heavenly realms. 13 Use every piece of God's armor to resist the enemy in the time of evil, so that after the battle you will still be standing firm. 14 Stand your ground, putting on the sturdy belt of truth and the body armor of God's righteousness. 15 For shoes, put on the peace that comes from the Good News, so that you will be fully prepared. 16 In every battle you will need faith as your shield to stop the fiery arrows aimed at you by Satan. 17 Put on salvation as your helmet, and take the sword of the Spirit, which is the word of God. 18 Pray at all times and on every occasion in the power of the Holy Spirit. Stay alert and be persistent in your prayers for all Christians everywhere.

Ephesians 3: 20-21 "Now glory be to God! By His mighty power at work within us, He is able to accomplish infinitely more than we would ever dare to ask or hope. May He be given glory in the church and in Christ Jesus forever and ever through endless ages. Amen."

The moment you accepted Christ into your heart you received a special gift of the Holy Spirit. The same spirit that raised Christ from the dead lives in you! There is MIGHTY POWER AT WORK WITHIN YOU! Because of the power of this spirit in you, God is able to accomplish infinitely more that we would ever dare or possibly be able to think, imagine, ask, or hope! This is an incredible revelation. God lives in you; Jesus lives in you, the Holy Spirit lives in you! WOW!!! We don't have to try to figure it all out because there is no possible way of conceiving with our human minds such a thing. All we must do is simply TRUST and OBEY. The Holy Spirit is a guide for our hearts and our conscience. Sometimes we can make it really complicated trying to figure it all out. Just listen to the Holy Spirit. He gently speaks to us and instructs us how to live. The Bible is God's written word. It is the best life instruction manual that will ever be written. When we tune into the spirit by feeding on God's Word and surrounding ourselves with positive and Godly information and people instead of feeding on the negative of the world, God is able to accomplish great things, greater than we could begin to imagine. This is true hope for us to stand on.

37 *1 Corinthians 9:24-26 "Remember that in a race everyone runs, but only one person gets the prize. You also much run in such a way that you will win. All athletes practice self-control. They do it to win a price that will fade away, but we do it for an eternal prize. So I run straight to the goal with purpose in every step..."*

Learning self-control has been a huge revelation for me. Growing up in an alcoholic home, I learned to get attention by creating drama and conflict. It surrounded me and enveloped me like a blanket. As children we model the behaviors that are around us. As we grow up we begin making discoveries about ourselves and then can make choices from those discoveries to the manner in which we are going to live. I truly believe that whatever we experience in life God has specifically designed for us to accomplish this purpose. He created each person uniquely, including the environment in which He has placed us in. There are no accidents. There are no coincidences. There are no surprises to God. He has given us free will to make our own choices but knows every thought and every word before it is even formed. We are personally responsible for our choices, our words and our thoughts. When we choose to walk in unforgiveness, we get stuck in playing a game of blame, shame and guilt; we choose a life of self-pity and destruction. We can choose to wallow in it and allow it to consume us or we can choose to live a life of peace and happiness. It is a choice. Many people don't realize they have a choice. They've been stuck for so long they don't know how to get out. I was one of those people. Thankfully the Lord placed wonderful people to minister to me and teach me that God loves me and that He has a purpose for my life. There is a reason He created me and He wants to accomplish His purpose in and through me. Once I began to understand this I was able to be more self-controlled. I chose not to react to every negative circumstance that came my way. I learned to choose to react in love and compassion. Every day I choose to live in my purpose and allow God to direct the steps in the path He has designed for me. You have a choice. My prayer is that you will allow God to work in your life to accomplish the will He has designed specifically for you. You are worthy of His love you are worthy of your purpose.

38

Philippians 4:13 For I can do everything with the help of Christ who gives me the strength I need.

As I write this I am overwhelmed with the revelation of God's love for me. As I have placed my faith in Him and have followed His path the Lord has truly given me strength and provided for me in ways I could not even imagine. One day I will write a book just on this verse and share all that God has done for me. The short version is that 18 short months ago I was dying. My lungs were shutting down due to severe asthma and my body was fighting itself with extreme allergic reactions to foods and chemicals both in my home and in the environment we live in. I couldn't lay flat in bed; I had to lay reclined in a chair for several weeks because if I laid flat I would stop breathing. I was in constant pain. My muscles would have such severe seizures my entire body would go into convulsions. My brain and muscles were not getting adequate oxygen. I could not stand on my own power without the use of a walker or walk with the aid of a family member. I felt I was dying and was ready to go home to be with the Lord when a friend called me with hope and shared some nutritional supplements that have completely transformed my life. Before my friend called, I was ready and prepared to die. In the midst of all of this I was able, because of the strength the Lord gave me, to complete and publish my first book. The Lord provided my friend's encouragement and the nutrition I needed to heal my body. The Lord has been so good to me. I have such a beautiful life and without His love and the love of my family and friends and their prayers I would not be here today. You would not be reading these words. Last year I accomplished so much and enjoyed momentous milestones of my life including watching my son Brady graduate from college and watching my daughter KayCee be married. I am continually learning to grow in my walk with the Lord and renewed health because of Christ's power and His love. As I continually focus on Him and walk in His grace and forgiveness my life is renewed. As I walk this journey and work towards cleaning out the trash can and listen to the new song of hope and love, my life is being healed. Friends, God wants to accomplish great things in you. You don't have to do it in your own strength and power. He is all you need. God wants to heal your life and give you a new song to live. You deserve to walk in the abundance of happiness and joy that God has purposed for you.

39

Isaiah 40:31 But those who wait on the LORD will find new strength. They will fly high on wings like eagles. They will run and not grow weary. They will walk and not faint.

What a wonderful promise to stand on for your life today! We live in a fast paced world that comes at us hard. We are constantly on the run striving to accomplish something. We run ourselves ragged doing our best to follow our dreams, accomplish our goals and achieve something in this life. We juggle the to-do list and the "branding irons in the fire." We become consumed with the things of this world and become weighted down, stressed, frustrated, angry and depressed. We need to stop and evaluate what our true purpose is. Who are we trying to accomplish all this for? What are we trying to accomplish? Why? If we measure our success according to the world's standards always being run by our broken records and worried about what others think and feel we will surely fail. We need to ask ourselves, "What does God want me to do? What are His desires?" When we truly step into our greatness of all God has created us to be and called us to accomplish then we will begin to live a life of true happiness, peace and abundance that our Heavenly Father desires us to have. When we are consumed with paying the bills and working ourselves to death to pay them striving to have everything "right now!" and living to accomplish a goal or a dream God does not intend for us to do, we are merely chasing our tails and accomplishing nothing spinning in a circle. Waiting on the Lord, for His perfect timing, listening to His Spirit and following His will for our lives we will renew our strength; we will rise up with wings like eagles. We will run and not grow weary we will walk and not be faint. We will achieve more with greater happiness doing His will, in His timing, His way.

40

Ephesians 1:15-19; 15 Therefore I also, after I heard of your faith in the Lord Jesus and your love for all the saints, 16 do not cease to give thanks for you, making mention of you in my prayers: 17 that the God of our Lord Jesus Christ, the Father of glory, may give to you the spirit of wisdom and revelation in the knowledge of Him, 18 the eyes of your understanding being enlightened; that you may know what is the hope of His calling, what are the riches of the glory of His inheritance in the saints, 19 and what is the exceeding greatness of His power toward us who believe, according to the working of His mighty power.

My sincere prayer is that through this book the Father of Glory will give you the spirit of wisdom and revelation in the knowledge of Him, that the eyes of your understanding be enlightened; that you may know what God's calling and purpose is for your life. I praise God for each and every person that is reading these words that you have received your personal revelation. Please know that I will be praying for you. I will not cease in giving God thanks for you. I love you, and GOD LOVES YOU! Thank you for the opportunity to share my heart with you. I pray you have been as blessed reading this as I have been in writing it with exceeding greatness. I pray that the Lord's mighty working power be increased in your life daily.

Rejoicing in Jesus,
Jamie Dearing

Psalm 119 1 Happy are people of integrity, who follow the law of the LORD. 2 Happy are those who obey His decrees and search for Him with all their hearts. 3 They do not compromise with evil, and they walk only in His paths. 4 You have charged us to keep Your commandments carefully. 5 Oh, that my actions would consistently reflect Your principles! 6 Then I will not be disgraced when I compare my life with Your commands. 7 When I learn Your righteous laws, I will thank You by living as I should! 8 I will obey Your principles. Please don't give up on me! 9 How can a young person stay pure? By obeying Your word and following its rules. 10 I have tried my best to find You -- don't let me wander from Your commands. 11 I have hidden Your word in my heart, that I might not sin against You. 12 Blessed are You, O LORD; teach me Your principles. 13 I have recited aloud all the laws You have given us. 14 I have rejoiced in Your decrees as much as in riches. 15 I will study Your commandments and reflect on Your ways. 16 I will delight in Your principles and not forget Your word. 17 Be good to Your servant, that I may live and obey Your word. 18 Open my eyes to see the wonderful truths in Your law. 19 I am but a foreigner here on earth; I need the guidance of Your commands. Don't hide them from me! 20 I am overwhelmed continually with a desire for Your laws. 21 You rebuke those cursed proud ones who wander from Your commands. 22 Don't let them scorn and insult me, for I have obeyed Your decrees. 23 Even princes sit and speak against me, but I will meditate on Your principles. 24 Your decrees please me; they give me wise advice. 25 I lie in the dust, completely discouraged; revive me by Your word. 26 I told You my plans, and You answered. Now teach me Your principles. 27 Help me understand the meaning of Your commandments, and I will meditate on Your wonderful miracles. 28 I weep with grief; encourage me by Your word. 29 Keep me from lying to myself; give me the privilege of knowing Your law. 30 I have chosen to be faithful; I have determined to live by

Your laws. 31 I cling to Your decrees. LORD, don't let me be put to shame! 32 If You will help me, I will run to follow Your commands. 33 Teach me, O LORD, to follow every one of Your principles. 34 Give me understanding and I will obey our law; I will put it into practice with all my heart. 35 Make me walk along the path of Your commands, for that is where my happiness is found. 36 Give me an eagerness for Your decrees; do not inflict me with love for money! 37 Turn my eyes from worthless things, and give me life through Your word. 38 Reassure me of Your promise, which is for those who honor You. 39 Help me abandon my shameful ways; Your laws are all I want in life. 40 I long to obey Your commandments! Renew my life with Your goodness. 41 LORD, give to me Your unfailing love, the salvation that You promised me. 42 Then I will have an answer for those who taunt me, for I trust in Your word. 43 Do not snatch Your word of truth from me, for my only hope is in Your laws. 44 I will keep on obeying Your law forever and forever. 45 I will walk in freedom, for I have devoted myself to Your commandments. 46 I will speak to kings about Your decrees, and I will not be ashamed. 47 How I delight in Your commands! How I love them! 48 I honor and love Your commands. I meditate on Your principles. 49 Remember Your promise to me, for it is my only hope. 50 Your promise revives me; it comforts me in all my troubles. 51 The proud hold me in utter contempt, but I do not turn away from Your law. 52 I meditate on Your age-old laws; O LORD, they comfort me. 53 I am furious with the wicked, those who reject Your law. 54 Your principles have been the music of my life throughout the years of my pilgrimage. 55 I reflect at night on who You are, O LORD, and I obey Your law because of this. 56 This is my happy way of life: obeying Your commandments. 57 LORD, You are mine! I promise to obey Your words! 58 With all my heart I want Your blessings. Be merciful just as You promised. 59 I pondered the direction of my life, and I turned to follow Your statutes. 60 I will hurry, without lingering, to obey Your commands. 61 Evil people try to drag me into sin, but I am firmly anchored to Your law. 62 At midnight I rise to thank You for Your just laws.

63 Anyone who fears You is my friend -- anyone who obeys Your commandments. 64 O LORD, the earth is full of Your unfailing love; teach me Your principles. 65 You have done many good things for me, LORD, just as You promised. 66 I believe in your commands; now teach me good judgment and knowledge. 67 I used to wander off until You disciplined me; but now I closely follow Your word. 68 You are good and do only good; teach me Your principles. 69 Arrogant people have made up lies about me, but in truth I obey Your commandments with all my heart. 70 Their hearts are dull and stupid, but I delight in Your law. 71 The suffering You sent was good for me, for it taught me to pay attention to Your principles. 72 Your law is more valuable to me than millions in gold and silver! 73 You made me; You created me. Now give me the sense to follow Your commands. 74 May all who fear You find in me a cause for joy, for I have put my hope in Your word. 75 I know, O LORD, that Your decisions are fair; You disciplined me because I needed it. 76 Now let Your unfailing love comfort me, just as You promised me, Your servant. 77 Surround me with Your tender mercies so I may live, for Your law is my delight. 78 Bring disgrace upon the arrogant people who lied about me; meanwhile, I will concentrate on Your commandments. 79 Let me be reconciled with all who fear You and know Your decrees. 80 May I be blameless in keeping Your principles; then I will never have to be ashamed. 81 I faint with longing for Your salvation; but I have put my hope in Your word. 82 My eyes are straining to see Your promises come true. When will You comfort me? 83 I am shriveled like a wineskin in the smoke, exhausted with waiting. But I cling to Your principles and obey them. 84 How long must I wait? When will You punish those who persecute me? 85 These arrogant people who hate Your law have dug deep pits for me to fall into. 86 All Your commands are trustworthy. Protect me from those who hunt me down without cause. 87 They almost finished me off, but I refused to abandon Your commandments. 88 In Your unfailing love, spare my life; then I can continue to obey Your decrees. 89 Forever, O LORD, Your word stands firm in heaven. 90 Your faithfulness extends to every generation, as enduring as the

earth You created. 91 Your laws remain true today, for everything serves Your plans. 92 If Your law hadn't sustained me with joy, I would have died in my misery. 93 I will never forget Your commandments, for You have used them to restore my joy and health. 94 I am Yours; save me! For I have applied myself to obey Your commandments. 95 Though the wicked hide along the way to kill me, I will quietly keep my mind on Your decrees. 96 Even perfection has its limits, but Your commands have no limit. 97 Oh, how I love Your law! I think about it all day long. 98 Your commands make me wiser than my enemies, for Your commands are my constant guide. 99 Yes, I have more insight than my teachers, for I am always thinking of Your decrees. 100 I am even wiser than my elders, for I have kept Your commandments. 101 I have refused to walk on any path of evil, that I may remain obedient to Your word. 102 I haven't turned away from Your laws, for you have taught me well. 103 How sweet are Your words to my taste; they are sweeter than honey. 104 Your commandments give me understanding; no wonder I hate every false way of life. 105 Your word is a lamp for my feet and a light for my path. 106 I've promised it once, and I'll promise again: I will obey Your wonderful laws. 107 I have suffered much, O LORD; restore my life again, just as You promised. 108 LORD, accept my grateful thanks and teach me Your laws. 109 My life constantly hangs in the balance, but I will not stop obeying Your law. 110 The wicked have set their traps for me along Your path, but I will not turn from Your commandments. 111 Your decrees are my treasure; they are truly my heart's delight. 112 I am determined to keep Your principles, even forever, to the very end. 113 I hate those who are undecided about You, but my choice is clear -- I love Your law. 114 You are my refuge and my shield; Your word is my only source of hope. 115 Get out of my life, you evil-minded people, for I intend to obey the commands of my God. 116 LORD, sustain me as You promised, that I may live! Do not let my hope be crushed. 117 Sustain me, and I will be saved; then I will meditate on Your principles continually. 118 But You have rejected all who stray from Your principles. They are only fooling themselves. 119 All the

wicked of the earth are the scum You skim off; no wonder I love to obey Your decrees! 120 I tremble in fear of You; I fear Your judgments. 121 Don't leave me to the mercy of my enemies, for I have done what is just and right. 122 Please guarantee a blessing for me. Don't let those who are arrogant oppress me!

123 My eyes strain to see Your deliverance, to see the truth of Your promise fulfilled. 124 I am Your servant; deal with me in unfailing love, and teach me Your principles. 125 Give discernment to me, Your servant; then I will understand Your decrees. 126 LORD, it is time for You to act, for these evil people have broken Your law. 127 Truly, I love Your commands more than gold, even the finest gold. 128 Truly, each of Your commandments is right. That is why I hate every false way. 129 Your decrees are wonderful. No wonder I obey them! 130 As Your words are taught, they give light; even the simple can understand them. 131 I open my mouth, panting expectantly, longing for Your commands. 132 Come and show me Your mercy, as You do for all who love Your name. 133 Guide my steps by Your word, so I will not be overcome by any evil. 134 Rescue me from the oppression of evil people; then I can obey Your commandments. 135 Look down on me with love; teach me all Your principles. 136 Rivers of tears gush from my eyes because people disobey Your law. 137 O LORD, You are righteous, and Your decisions are fair. 138 Your decrees are perfect; they are entirely worthy of our trust. 139 I am overwhelmed with rage, for my enemies have disregarded Your words. 140 Your promises have been thoroughly tested; that is why I love them so much. 141 I am insignificant and despised, but I don't forget Your commandments. 142 Your justice is eternal, and Your law is perfectly true. 143 As pressure and stress bear down on me, I find joy in Your commands. 144 Your decrees are always fair; help me to understand them, that I may live. 145 I pray with all my heart; answer me, LORD! I will obey Your principles. 146 I cry out to you; save me, that I may obey Your decrees. 147 I rise early, before the sun is up; I cry out for help and put my hope in Your words. 148 I stay awake through the night, thinking

about Your promise. 149 In Your faithful love, O LORD, hear my cry; in Your justice, save my life. 150 Those lawless people are coming near to attack me; they live far from Your law. 151 But You are near, O LORD, and all Your commands are true. 152 I have known from my earliest days that Your decrees never change. 153 Look down upon my sorrows and rescue me, for I have not forgotten Your law. 154 Argue my case; take my side! Protect my life as You promised. 155 The wicked are far from salvation, for they do not bother with Your principles. 156 LORD, how great is your mercy; in Your justice, give me back my life. 157 Many persecute and trouble me, yet I have not swerved from Your decrees. 158 I hate these traitors because they care nothing for Your word. 159 See how I love Your commandments, LORD. Give back my life because of Your unfailing love. 160 All Your words are true; all Your just laws will stand forever. 161 Powerful people harass me without cause, but my heart trembles only at Your word. 162 I rejoice in Your word like one who finds a great treasure. 163 I hate and abhor all falsehood, but I love Your law. 164 I will praise You seven times a day because all Your laws are just. 165 Those who love Your law have great peace and do not stumble. 166 I long for Your salvation, LORD, so I have obeyed Your commands. 167 I have obeyed Your decrees, and I love them very much. 168 Yes, I obey Your commandments and decrees, because You know everything I do. 169 O LORD, listen to my cry; give me the discerning mind You promised. 170 Listen to my prayer; rescue me as you promised. 171 Let my lips burst forth with praise, for You have taught me Your principles. 172 Let my tongue sing about Your word, for all Your commands are right. 173 Stand ready to help me, for I have chosen to follow Your commandments. 174 O LORD, I have longed for Your salvation, and Your law is my delight. 175 Let me live so I can praise You, and may Your laws sustain me. 176 I have wandered away like a lost sheep; come and find me, for I have not forgotten Your commands.

I would like to encourage you today, wherever you find yourself, no matter the circumstance, God loves you and He is with you! He will provide for you and help you as long as you surrender to Him. You have been able to read the words written in this book because of countless prayers that have been answered and miracles that have been performed in and through me. I love you and am blessed beyond measure to share the gifts God has created specifically in me to share with you to bless your life. May you be blessed more and more as the revelation of God's love dwells in your heart, your spirit and your mind. To God, you are a rock star! You shine brightly! He has a picture of you on His refrigerator in Heaven and a poster of you on His bedroom wall! He thinks about you all the time and delights in all you are and all you do! Allow yourself to sing a new song of praise and thanksgiving to Him for all that He is all that He has done; and all He will do for you. Your destiny is just one choice, one decision away. Start today by believing you can create the life God has planned for you!

2 Timothy 1:7 NLT
For God has not given us a spirit of fear and timidity, but of power, love, and self-discipline.

THERE IS A PLAN IN THIS BOOK TO HAVE 'ETERNAL SALVATION'

READ THE FOLLOWING SCRIPTURES AND UNDERSTAND WHAT THE MEANING OF ETERNAL LIFE IS

JOHN 3:16
ROMANS 3: 10,11
ROMANS 3:23
ROMANS 10: 9,10

If you wish to have a personal relationship with Jesus Christ and wish to accept Him as your Lord and Savior so that you will receive the gift of eternal life, simply pray this prayer: "Lord Jesus, I am a sinner. I confess my sin to you. I believe that you died for me and shed your blood so that I may be redeemed and have eternal life with you. I believe that you were raised from the dead and sit at the right hand of my creator, and our Heavenly Father. Lord I ask that you come and live in me through the power of the Holy Spirit. I thank you for your sacrifice and I give my heart and my life over to you, in Jesus Name I pray, AMEN!!"
HALLELUJAH!!! PRAISE GOD!! CONGRATULATIONS FOR MAKING THE BEST CHOICE OF YOUR LIFE!! You are now born again!! Welcome to the family! Now confess to a friend that JESUS IS YOUR LORD AND SAVIOR!!!

Ruby Langley grew up riding horses competing in 4-h, W.A.S.H.E.T., and Rodeo. Being raised in the ranch lifestyle is what has shaped her vision as an artist. At the age of 12 Ruby fell in love with the camera when she got her hands on her dad's pentax K1000 film camera. When she was 16 she got the opportunity to apprentice with a PRCA Photographer for the summer. That summer, Ruby decided to go to school for photography and make a career out of her passion. In June of 2012, Ruby graduated from Spokane Falls Community College with a Associates in Applied Science majoring in Photography. Ruby Langley is the owner and photographer of Ruby Images. Ruby Images specializes in Equine event and portrait photography, and fine art western vignettes.

The images in this book were created by Ruby Langley for the Glory of the Most High.

If you would like to view or purchase any of the photographs in this book you can do so at www.RubyImages.net